I0539860

Daddy's Package
Copyright © 2025 by C.C. Danforth
All rights reserved.

No part of this book may be reproduced, stored in a retrieval system, or transmitted in any form or by any means—electronic, mechanical, photocopying, recording, or otherwise—without the prior written permission of the publisher, except in the case of brief quotations used in reviews or articles.

ISBN: 979-8-218-58740-6
Illustrations by: Cornelius Kuncana
First Edition, 2025

Printed in the United States of America
This book is intended for entertainment purposes only and is not suitable for children. It contains humor and innuendos designed for adults with a sense of humor.

For inquiries, please contact:
CassieCDanforth@gmail.com

C.C. Danforth

Mommy loves getting mail and packages galore!
They come in all shapes and sizes.
She waits for them by the door.

She says she loves all packages; the size doesn't matter. She likes the short ones, the long ones, and those that are fatter.

Sometimes they're brown,
and sometimes they're white.
The brown ones are always bigger—
they fill her with delight.

One day, Daddy surprised her with a package so small.
He tucked it away, barely visible at all.

Mommy took Daddy's package and shook it around.
Oops! She shook too hard, and her gift fell to the ground.

Daddy sighed as it fell to the floor.
It broke and splattered—the package was no more.

Daddy helped Mommy clean up the mess.
It was all over her legs, her face, and her chest.

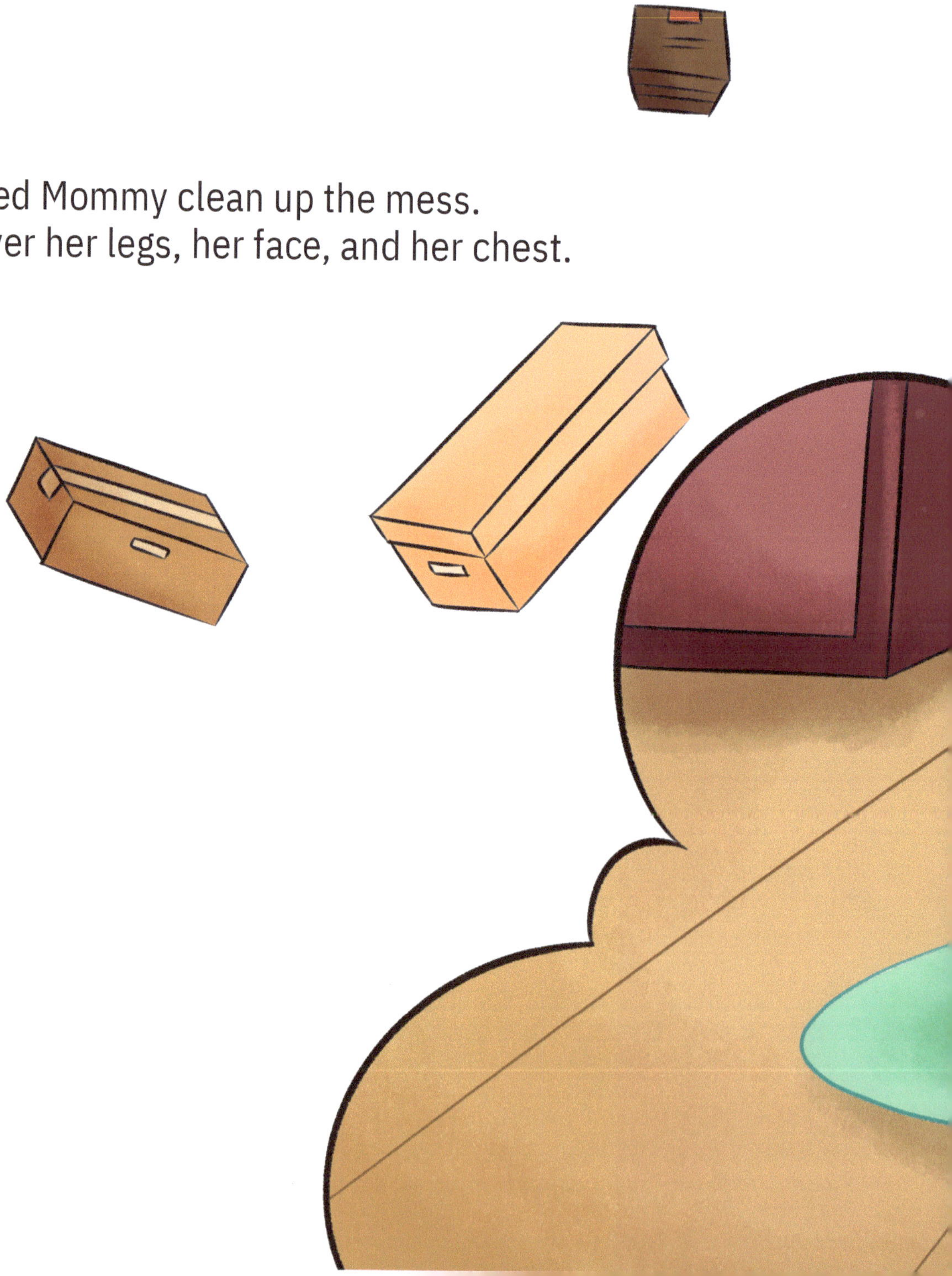

"Accidents happen,"
Daddy said, not
the least bit mad.

"Next time, we'll be more careful. No need to be sad!"

Later that evening, Mommy was tired,
She thought about the day and all that had transpired.

Just as she closed her eyes for a nap, Daddy appeared with another package on his lap.

Mommy's eyes sparkled; she couldn't believe her sight—
Another surprise from Daddy—what a delight!

She took it gently, with a smile so wide.
It only took a few seconds to see what was inside.

"I love it so much! Thank you!" she said,
As she gave him a big hug and kissed his head.

Their love is so strong, no need for pretending.
Together forever—a happy ending!

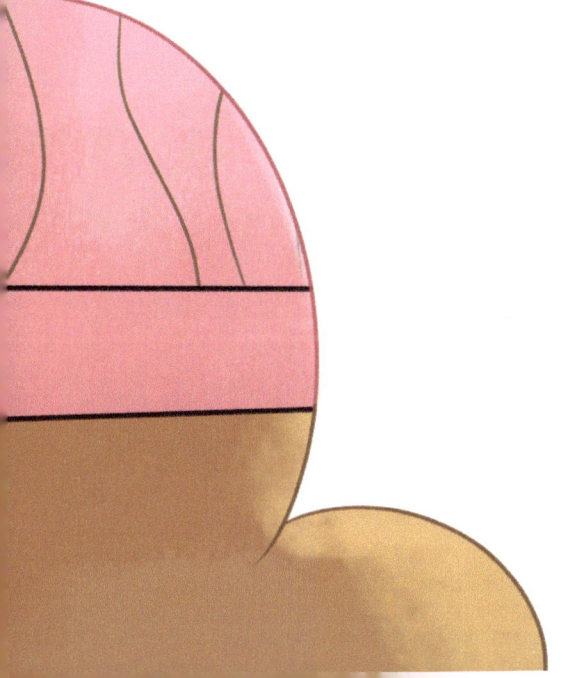

www.ingramcontent.com/pod-product-compliance
Lightning Source LLC
Chambersburg PA
CBHW041436120626
46547CB00002B/236